# Of Angels And Demons

# Of Angels And Demons

Artemis

Copyright © 2019 by Artemis Poetry

All rights reserved.

Published in the United States of America by Kindle Direct Publishing, Seattle, Washington. No part of this book may be used or reproduced in any manner whatsoever without written permission except in the case of reprints in the context of reviews.

Library of Congress Cataloging-in-Publication Data is available upon request.

ISBN-13: 978-0-578-47618-6

Printed in the United States of America

10 9 8 7 6 5 4 3 2 1

Thank you to those who continue to inspire me, motivate me, and love me. I am forever thankful for those of you who stood by and continue to stand by me while I figure out this whole thing called life. You are my muses, my loves, and my lights.

And to the many authors and poets before me, I don't think I can even put myself in your category, but I thank you for your never ending inspiration, pushing me to strive for better and more honest words, and for giving a voice to the voiceless.

And to the little girls and boys out there sitting alone in the dark, please know that I am there with you, and hope that this book can serve as a light for you.

And to ART and MEB, thank you for teaching me about love, tenacity, grit, and what it means to speak up for myself and others. You are always with me.

# Of Angels And Demons

"If you want the moon, do not hide from the night. If you want a rose, do not run from the thorns. If you want love, do not hide from yourself."
-Rumi

I'm not entirely sure how it even happened
It was like being hit by something
And only noticing a small ache
An ache that I could ignore
And did for months
Only to wake up one day feeling every ounce of pain
that had built up
I tried to hide it
Tried to ignore it
But no matter how hard I tried it fought back harder
It became my own personal nightmare
A demon that taunted me all hours of the day and
night

Strangers creep into my mind
And I am fearful
What's worse is that they come with guests I have seen many times before
I didn't know my demons had friends
I didn't know that they would bring their friends to taunt me more

It lived somewhere deep inside
In a cavern I had long since hidden and tried to forget
The only problem is that the deeper you try to bury
something the more it wants to surface
It's almost like it knows that you are trying
And it can't let you win

My eyes ache for relief
It's been hours since the tears began
And I haven't seen a reprieve yet
By now I have cried an ocean of pain and a river of sorrow
By now my pain could topple mountains
My sadness destroy cities
And my anger ravage entire empires

Somehow it seeped into me this anger
I didn't know could exist
This hatred born of pain
And this fear born of loneliness

The ice in my bones cracks under the fire of my skin
The constant burning and freezing leaves me floating in
my pain

Its words are always with me
It whispers to me when the world is loud
And screams to me when my world is too quiet for comfort
My own personal lullaby
A mental fortress of my own design
Words unchanged throughout time
A faith tested but left unharmed

Questioning when and how it all began led me to a
question I never planned on asking myself
Why

I want to have a why to help explain all of this
But I don't know if one even exists
And if it does do I want to know if the reason is
because of something I did

I don't see how I am ever going to be able to accept this
when it fundamentally goes against everything I am
I can't accept it
And I don't think I want to either because that is the
same as admitting failure
Admitting that I let this defeat me
How am I supposed to not hate myself if that happens
How am I supposed to live a life
And want to live it if I am that angry at myself
If I can't fight my own demons and keep them at bay

I know that people say this isn't my fault
And that I shouldn't blame myself because I didn't
choose for this to happen
But that doesn't make me feel any better

I should be stronger than this
I should be able to move past this
And be better
I shouldn't let this take control of me and ruin my life

Was I destined to burn
Or did I simply get too close to the sun

Tears stream down my face
And I forget just for a moment about my walls
My shield lessens but for a moment
Before rising up again to ward off the day

Hunger for that feeling again
That feeling of self
Knowing who I am and what I want
Numbed by my own feelings
Overwhelmed by the thoughts rushing through my mind
I feel the flames rise up to greet me
Whispering hello like an old friend
Then all of a sudden I am burning, burning alive
Quick I need water
Water will help
The fire is gone
For the moment
But now I am drowning
Gasping for a breath that I can't seem to catch
The breath that holds who I used to be
If only I could rise above the waves
And drift far enough from the flames
Maybe then I would find my feet on solid ground
A chance to breathe
A chance to live

What is it about the night
The dark that brings out my tears, my pain
I guess it makes sense to be your most vulnerable when
you can hide from the world
When your pillow can become the shield that protects
others from your screams
And the night sky your greatest confidant
Maybe the darkness strips of us everything the day
builds up in us
We release everything
And try to put it away as we sleep
With the hope that when we wake the morning light
will be a welcomed friend
A sign of relief

There is a part of me that thinks no matter what
I will always be that scared little girl hiding beneath her
covers

What if for once I actually told you the truth
Would it scare you away

Somehow I have been burning since the beginning
But now I am freezing too

I can't bear to bare my heart so instead I bare my skin
And build a mosaic of scars upon scars
Slowly hardening into my armor

I've crafted my story
With a collection of woven and tattered lies
Disguised as the most beautiful tapestry

Do your worst
My scars have hardened me so much
That I haven't felt anything in years

Am I brave enough to face the demons from my own mind

I'm bleeding out just to feel this life

Caught in a storm of my own making
Caught in a storm I can't stop
I didn't mean to start it
It started while I was sleeping
Crept up on me and caught me by surprise
Now I am left drenched, cold, and struggling to see
through the rain

Losing yourself within your own mind is probably the most frightening way to fall apart

Drifting in and out of consciousness
Only partially aware of what is going on around you
But then the light flickers
And you realize that your body has been awake the whole time
But your mind remains paused
Numb to the outside

Reminded that the sun, the moon, and the morning
birds don't even flinch if you don't wake
Your existence is small to them
If you want them to acknowledge you, you must stop
them in their tracks
And greet them as if you are as essential to the world
To the beginning and ending of the day as they are

It's strange
I see her
I know her
I am her
Well I was her
Now I stare at her like people stare at their old baby photos
Having to remind themselves that they were once that person
But now someone new stands in that same place
For most people that new person is good
A newer, truer version of themselves
The self they have discovered somewhere along the road
For me it's different
The person standing here now isn't truer
Better
Or a culmination of experiences
This person is what is left
The shell of what is left of the girl in the mirror
Road rash
Battle torn
And barely hanging on

Lying everyday
Masking the demons that lurk just under the surface
Spending all day fighting to keep them down
Low enough that no one can see
Wondering if the day will come when they burst out
And the world is left speechless
Speechless by the darkness
Speechless by my pain
And even more speechless at my constant lies and deception
My ability to change what people see
Make you see the mask that I paint everyday
Standing in the mirror preparing myself like I am going to war
Going undercover
In a way I am I guess
Thinking of new tactics
New ways to distract
Persuade
And manipulate the people around me so that they don't notice
Because noticing means questions
Questions that I can't answer
Though I desperately ache to
Projecting the perfect hologram of who I should be
Who they want to know me as
Constantly
Cautiously
And consciously aware of everything around me

But if you looked on the inside
You would see a little girl sitting crouched in the corner
of the room
Just hoping that the beauty of the stained glass
windows she's painting will convince people that they
don't need to look in
That everything is fine

Hunting for the person I used to be
I'm not saying she was perfect in fact far from it
She was also broken
But she could at least hide it
And pretend to be strong on the outside
That is the person I miss
The person who could
Could do anything

I can hear the wolves howling out my window
beckoning me to come home to join the darkness

Standing next to the water
Watching the incoming waves come rolling in
And leave dragging with them sand, shells, and whatever they want to take
All the while I am left untouched
The water may wash me, but it won't submerge me
It won't baptize me and lead me to a new life
Yearning for the water to take me too
Take me anywhere but here
Take me back to her
Back to who I was
Leave me tossing in the surf as the current replaces all the pain and confusion with the remnants of her
Hoping that when I emerge from the depths she will be with me
That I will be her again
Or a better version even
A version polished and strengthened by the sea
By the claiming and all consuming nature of the water

Finding solace in the silence
Knowing that the quiet won't turn on you
Feeling comfort in the empty because after this long
It is what feels normal to you
An odd sense of comfort in the pain
The pain you feel everyday
The pain that reminds you
You are alive
You are still here
While that is terrifying
It is also one of the only constant, you can count on
And right now consistency is the closest you have to normalcy
And normalcy is the closest to feeling good
While nothing about this is normal or feels good
It is what you have
The same
Nothing unexpected
Nothing new to hurt you
Or at least you hope
Tomorrow could change all of that

People ask me what it feels like
Well actually that's a lie
Most people don't ask a damn thing
For the ones who do
Or the ones who want some kind of explanation
I try my best to describe the feelings
The pain of my skin being burned from my body
The feeling of drowning
An inability to catch my breath
At the same time everything around me is dark and wet and I can't see anything
It feels like getting continually punched in the gut
To the point that you eventually embrace
And even normalize the abuse
Because it provides some kind of consistency
And with nothing to hold onto, it is something to expect
Something in a twisted way to look forward to

Sometimes I wonder if they even notice
If they even notice that I am slipping away more and more each day

A prisoner
A slave
Trapped by her own thoughts and feelings
They seem to swarm around her all the time
So fast that they suck the oxygen out of the room
Unable to breath she collapses and waits for the end

Drifting in and out of consciousness hoping that one of
the moments will stick
Just give me stability
I will settle for whatever you can give me at this point

Hands clasped
Blood running
Tracing the lines that hold me together

Head bowed
Hands clasped
Pressed against my forehead
Pleading for any help
Please, I scream
Whatever you want I'll do it
Just make it stop please
What did I do to deserve this
Do I deserve this
Asking the same questions everyday
Somehow always hoping that something will change
That someone will hear
That someone will help
But nothing ever happens
But I still keep going
Some may call that hope
But it seems closer to insanity to me
My own never-ending tortuous record
Playing so only I can hear it

Creeping in so quietly you almost miss it
You see but pay it no real attention until it has
swallowed you whole

Submerged in fire and washed in pain
Carved up by feelings and words never meant to exist
Left raw, broken, and beaten on the floor
You lay still because you know there's more

Silence comforts
Silence terrorizes
Silence reminds
Silence remembers

Static
A mere annoyance on occasion
Whispers
Noticeable, but nothing to really worry about
Talking
It's here but you pretend it isn't
Maybe if you pretend they will stop
Shouting
Just try harder
Cover your ears
Block it out
Screaming
No more
It is too loud
Too much
Too everything
You collapse

Fists clenched
Palms sweaty
Heart racing
Cheeks flushing
All at once I am under attack
Fighting to get out
To run away
I keep looking for my attacker and see no one
But the mirror never fails to remind me that I am my own abuser

Dragging around the corpse of my former self
Hoping that the people who knew her will catch a glimpse
And tell themselves that even though I am not her that they should stay anyway

Muscles clenched
Skin starts to itch
Heart is racing
Hands start to sweat
The lights begin to blur
Just hold on I tell myself
Just breath I tell myself
It can't last forever I repeat in my head
But she screams over my voice and laughs at me as I try to stay alive

My pillow is soaked
Soaked from a never ending stream of tears
Soaked with saliva from my attempts to muffle my screams
Weak and broken until finally I crumble under the weight of the pain and my mind takes a momentary respite in sleeping
But when I wake my puffy eyes, my soar throat, my tired soul, all remind me that last night wasn't a dream
But rather my own personal wide-awake nightmare

Crying out for help
But my screams are drowned out by the smile fixed
across my face
The smile I put on to let the world know that I am ok
To let the world know that I am not broken
But those are all lies

Clamoring for some ounce of clarity, and semblance of normalcy
But I honestly don't know if I even remember what those feel like anymore

Crafting the perfect responses
Manufacturing the perfect smile
Anything to disguise myself
To pretend that everything is fine

Walking around dazed, barely breathing, barely surviving
But very few people even raise their eyes to notice
Because no one wants to see the darkness in someone else

I stare down at them and it almost feels like they aren't real
Like they aren't mine
A sort of outer body experience mixed with a dose of existential thinking
But I do know that they are mine
It's just that the detachment is so much more real some days
So much more all encompassing

Ripped apart at the seams
Held together by safety pins
Maybe if I position them just right no one will see them
That's right if I hide them in the folds of my life, of my personality, of my smile no one will see
But maybe that is the problem
No one does see and I have hidden it for so long that I am not sure I even see its true depth anymore

Strangled by my own thoughts
Chained to the floor by my own feelings
Unable to move
Gasping for breath while my brain tells my lungs to stop
To bow out
Trying to stay alive in a body that feels like death
A body that wants to die
There is nothing alive about that
Nothing living, this is the walking dead

It's like being punched straight through your chest
This soul crushing completely empty feeling in your soul
Both a visceral and existential feeling of loss
And I know it's there because the wind never stops gushing through the hole in my chest
I am constantly fighting the gale force winds that try to bury me beneath the Earth
Every dark thought that enters my mind comes from that hole
Comes from somewhere deep in the darkness of my own personal abyss
Every moment of light or a semblance of such is constantly stolen by the vast emptiness
Like a black hole swallowing up anything that enters its path
It takes no prisoners only eradicating unassumingly
The only prisoner in this equation is me

The darkness invades my mind
The numbness invades my body
Before I know it my body isn't mine anymore
It belongs to it
I am somewhere hiding in the corner of my mind with my eyes closed and my ears covered
Hoping just hoping that it will leave me alone
The longer it attacks me the further away I seem
Floating somewhere else
Still tethered to this mind and body but completely detached

My thoughts are like puzzle pieces only without edges
They are swirling around in a world without context,
without a foundation, without clarity
But the longer I stare at their picture the more confused
I become

Its spirit calls to me
Calls me in a way that I can feel in my bones
I can feel it on my skin
In my soul
It reminds me that we have been apart for too long
My skin begins to wrinkle, leather, and shrivel
My feet lose the quickness of their step
My voice loses its power
My breath loses its need
My soul loses its way

They tell you to pull yourself up by your bootstraps
But what do you do if you have no straps to pull
Or worse your boots have been stolen
And you are left standing in a puddle of the remnants
of a life not lived

Taming the darkness to give the light a chance
But what if my darkness is what gives the light the confidence to shine

Time has left me bewildered, blinded, and broken
The more days that pass the quicker the weeks seem to go
The days drag on, but then I blink and 3 months have passed
Wasting my life away staring at a clock that only reminds me of the war that I am still losing

The emptiness consumes me
The blackness swallows me whole
The void drains every ounce of life in me
Every time I try to breath my lungs burn at their inability to capture air
Every time I open my eyes they are greeted with nothing but darkness
A nothingness that has taken everything from me

Saying goodbye to one of the last pieces of myself I could recognize

I can taste it on my tongue
Like sharp metal warning me of something wrong
My lungs start to struggle
I can't catch my breath
My palms start to sweat
My skin starts to heat up
I am drowning and burning alive all at once
And people ask me what's wrong
What am I supposed to tell them

Dreaming of a day where the pain and demons don't
greet my eyes before the light does
I hope that day is soon
I don't know how many of the bad days I have left in
me

It's been so long that I don't even remember where I left you

I've spent so long feeling so far from any sense of
normalcy
Or the closest I had ever come to it
That I can't even imagine getting out of this
I can't imagine not feeling like this
I can't picture how to get out of it
I can't even tell you where I would want to end up if all
of this were to change
Because the longer it goes on the harder it becomes for
me to remember what it used to be like
What I used to be like

No one understands
I mean how could they
I don't even really understand it
All I know is that every waking moment I feel like I am drowning
Like I can't breathe
I feel like someone has punched me in the chest
And sucked all the oxygen out of the room and they still expect me to survive

Stepping outside reminds me just how much I don't feel normal
Just how much I don't feel a part of that world

Somewhere along the way I lost you
I'm not even entirely sure if you were ever truly there
Maybe you were more of a shadow than anything else
All I know is that I hope that one day I find my way back to you
Or just to you at all

The ideas enter my mind in waves
But just as quick as turning off a light they are gone
My mind twists them
Warps them
And tells me that they are wrong
That it is all wrong

Somewhere along the way I tripped
And instead of getting back up I sank into the Earth
The farther down I sink the farther ahead others get

Not knowing what to do
Not knowing what decisions to make
How can I know when everything feels wrong

No idea of how I got here
And even less idea of how to get out

I feel like I am drifting deeper and deeper
Farther away with each passing day
But I don't know how to hold on
And no one seems to know how to reach out and grab
me

I have grown so careful in how I show it to others
I have learned the hard way that people only have a
certain capacity for another's pain
And once that threshold is reached they check out
To me it is just easier not to show them
Not to tell them
That way they never know
And never check out
I am the one who checks out

Everything around me feels like it is spinning out of control
And I am still straining to try and see where I am

I feel like my lungs are burning
Burning from holding my breath
Trying to stop my panicking
Trying to stop my heart from racing
But it's not just that
My lungs burn from the screams inside of them
The screams trapped trying to come out
Tearing and shredded just hoping that I burst at the seams and they can escape
I try everything I can to quiet them
But even if no one else hears them they are my own personal alarm
Whose sole job is to push me over the edge

The more hours that tick by the farther I shrink away
The farther I shrink into myself
Any attempt to save whatever last slivers of myself remain

More and more each day my body and mind grow
weaker and weaker
And more and more exhausted
Trying to muster up energy to even join the day is a
struggle of epic proportions

Fighting a battle where the enemy is the same as the soldier

Clamoring to find some sense of why
Searching for any semblance of who I used to be
But it seems like I no longer even know who that is
Or what she looks like

I try to sleep but it creeps in no matter how hard I try
It's like a smoke that engulfs me
Slowly strangling the breath out of me

The flames rise up and I can feel my skin starting to
scream
The hotter it gets the quieter I become
And the more I retreat into myself
This is the only way I know to survive

As I sit alone my mind begins to wander
But the wandering is never good
It wanders into the darkness
Into the storm
And I feel myself slipping further and further away
from this world

I have cried so much that now the tears are permanently dried to my face

They ask you where is your pain
They ask you to rate your pain
They ask you to explain what it feels like
How do you explain without sounding ridiculous that
you feel pain in every inch of your body
You feel pain in your deepest darkest most protected
crevices to the outermost portions of your skin that
burn as if the air is acid

I catch a glimpse of you in the mirror
And I am reminded that in some way you are still here
But in all the ways that matter you are gone

The silence has become both my constant companion
and my most ardent tormenter

My worst enemies are all of my own creation
Except I didn't even know I was creating them
I didn't know I was becoming a host to an army of my own demons
Crafted just perfectly to ensure my demise

The world outside my window passes by faster and
faster each day
And before long all I see is a blur

Craving sanity in a world of insanity
Craving clarity in a world of confusion
Craving calm in a world of chaos

I find myself simultaneously captivated and terrified by
the detached feeling that separates me from the world
On one level it is interesting to look around and feel as
if you aren't present
As if you are watching some kind of bizarre movie
But on the other hand everything is far more terrifying
when you feel like there is nothing holding you here
And each day you drift further and further away

The more days that pass the deeper and deeper she gets buried
And I worry that if I ever get to her
Will she have succumbed to the darkness and lack of oxygen and perished forever

I have become so accustomed to these feelings that they
have become my most present and consuming
relationship

Drenched in feelings that I don't want
Drowning in thoughts I can't escape
Blinded by the force in which they attack my every cell

The marks on my skin remind me of my struggle
The moment in the morning when my feelings began to overwhelm me
And I look down to find my nails digging into my skin
The pain serves as a temporary distraction from the swirling of my thoughts
And the fear that bubbles up inside me like hot lava
But before long even that distraction is gone
And I am alone again with my thoughts

I feel it draining out of me
Like water dripping out of a faucet or my blood dripping from my fingertips
My identity, my strength, everything I had worked for
Slowly trickling out of me as I desperately ache for their return
The problem is that their loss makes it harder for me to fight to get them back

I honestly don't know how I got here
Somewhere within these days I slowly and all at once
drifted away

Tempted by people who say they want to know
Tempted by people who say they can take it
But in my experience none of that is the case

Trying to find a place in my mind where I can escape
Except the problem is that my mind is what I am trying
to escape

Strangled by my own thoughts I search for the breath I
need to survive
But my body refuses to accept any air

It feels like drowning and simultaneously being burned alive
It feels like sitting in a warm bath in dim lighting
Being lured in by a false sense of security
But then the drain plug is pulled
And you stay there in the dark slowly feeling every ounce of security and peace and joy leaving your body
Until there is nothing left but a shell
And that shell is you
Broken, hollow, and in pain
Shivering and naked in the dark
Truly alone
And then the light comes back on but it isn't refreshing or hopeful
It is blinding because now you see yourself
You see yourself naked, shaking, and hopeless with the only water in the tub streaming down your cheeks

Of all of the feelings that seem to ravage my mind and
body my own detachment may scare me the most
There is something terrifying about not feeling present
in your own life
Questioning every little thing until you find yourself
cycling through a flurry or existential thoughts and
feelings that only lead to a dark place

I find it ironic that people keep telling me to stay
positive or to remain optimistic
Like I somehow have control over that
I mean let's be real for a second if I could do those
things then I wouldn't even be in this mess in the first
place

Somewhere along the way I lost you
And I am scared that without you no one will recognize
me
Will they like the piece that is just me

I feel like that little kid who fell down and scraped their knee
Except it seems that the gravel has dug itself into my soul
I can feel it grating against my bones
Blocking my flowing blood
And pinching my nerves reminding me that something is wrong
Something wrong happened

Screaming into my pillow
Tears run down my face
I am trying to muffle my own cries while sucking in the fabric drenched with my pain

I used to think that the water could wash away my problems
Even just temporarily
Wash away the thoughts of my problems may be a more accurate way of explaining the powers I always felt the sea had
But now I doubt even the comforting chill and cleansing bath of the ocean could blur these thoughts from my mind
Let alone heal me

Such an exquisite pain is that which comes from within our own souls

I think I have hidden my real face for so long now that even when I look in the mirror I see the mask

Living a life with my hands tied behind my back

Caught in a fire of my own design
I thought it would protect me
But now I am left burnt beyond recognition

Hunting for the girl I left behind
But sometimes I wonder was she ever really there

The years of scars have made my skin and heart so thick that I worry no one will be able to reach it without cutting so deep that I lose everything

Trapped in a prison of my own design
But I didn't mean to make a prison
I meant to make a castle
A fortress to protect myself
But somehow I have protected the world from me
instead of the opposite

Maybe she could fix herself
I mean after all she was the one who broke herself
I know it wasn't really her fault
But she needed someone to blame other than random chance
This way she had an actual enemy
Something to target and fight against
But what do you do if your enemy
The thing you are trying to destroy
Is the same thing you are trying to save

Her pride would either save her or destroy her
Only time would tell which

The blood that ran through her veins was drenched in a
history of fighting
Fighting in wars, for land, for family, for life
But now she was fighting for something new
She was fighting herself to save herself

Trapped in a world where no one seems to know my real name
And I can't seem to speak up loud enough to tell them

Controlled by a demon that only I can hear
That only I can feel
And only I can see

My camouflage has become what people think is my real face
And now I begin to wonder if I am starting to believe my own lies

What's left of me you ask
Honestly I don't know
Right now it feels like not much

The blackness seeps into my soul like a cancer invading the body
Taking hold, growing uncontrollably, hiding its true face
Hopefully it won't be too late this time

A prisoner in your own mind
In your own body
A refugee when you venture into the world
Fleeing your own torment
Or at least trying
Hoping that those buzzing around provide you some aid
They may not know that they are humanitarians
But you know that without them you would drown in your own endless darkness

Sweet like rain
Loud like thunder
Passionate
And burning like a just struck match
And strong like a mountain
She has battled her whole life
She has faced demons that only exist in stories
And somehow she could always win the fight
She was strategic
Smart
Tenacious
And had something to prove
But this demon was different
This demon knew her
This demon was her
It had been lurking, hiding, and growing for so long that she didn't expect it to overtake her
It had just always been there somewhere in the back of her mind
Clawing its way out
You will never be able to understand her pain because even she doesn't understand it
You wonder why she doesn't share
But why would she want to put the blackest and most consuming of darkness upon the people she loves most
Alone
Yes being alone is easier
Well it's not
But being alone means no one else has to fight
She is so used to being the only soldier
That she wears her armor to bed
They aren't ready
They don't know what is coming
And they shouldn't have to
Let them continue to live in the good part of the stories
The parts where the princess is saved
And the heroes always win

I need you to love me a little harder right now because
somewhere along the way I forgot how to
If I ever knew to begin with

Pulsing through my skin
Racing through my blood
Sparking each cell in my body
Somehow it always brings me back from the edge
Always keeps me alive

I thought I had prepared for everything
But I couldn't have ever planned for this

The burning is a reminder that while this hasn't killed me yet it is still trying to

I wonder if I will ever get better
And if I do will I know it when I see it
I mean it has been so long now that I may not
remember what a good day feels like
And I may not even recognize it

My strength runs deep like the roots of the old oak I
grew up under
But just like that oak my roots are fragile
Living within a delicate balance between life and death
One drought and I start to wither
One wrong storm and my branches begin to crack from
the beatings of the world
I begin to wonder how many more storms this old oak
can weather before it sinks back into the Earth

Maybe just maybe this time will be more
This time will be different

I hope that one day the little girl I left behind finally
catches up with me
Because she had a clarity and joy that I yearn to have
again

Shedding pieces I have come to value
Pieces I have come to rely on
Maybe their removal will usher in a new hope
A new promise for tomorrow

Somewhere out there I hope there is a little girl sitting in her room realizing that she doesn't have to live like this
That she doesn't have to hide, to lie, or to pretend that she is or feels something she doesn't
My hope is that that girl grows up to realize that everything about her is what makes her who she is
Even if she doesn't want others to see it
I hope she knows that even if we never meet that I am rooting for her
From one hider to another

I saw the look on her face when I said it
It was like for the first time she was actually hearing me
For the first time she actually understood on some level
what I was describing to her
She finally on some small level understood my pain,
even if for a brief moment
I guess that's progress
And progress means that I don't have to do this alone
And that is something I am okay with

Something about the coolness of the night air reminds
me that despite all of this there is something alive
Something still feeling in me

I always thought I was strong
I mean at least I was able to portray that on the outside
Keep my demons and pain in check
Create a life and a face that the world can handle seeing
Something that allows you to keep fighting and getting
up every morning
Maybe if there is an end to this
Maybe if the fighting is worth it I will be stronger for it

Somewhere underneath this I hope a part of her is still
alive
Even just a cell left
Anything to use to hold on
Something to grab onto for life

To the little girl within me scared and unsure
Just know that one day you will find that all of this has
made you the fiercest of storms

My cracks have cracks
And my breaks have breaks
I just hope that one day instead of feeling like darkness
leaks out through my fissures
I feel like the most blinding of lights erupting from
within

She was drowning in herself until one day she took a
breath
And everything changed

Sometimes I wonder if there is someone out there going through the same thing I am
Am I the only one who seems to have lost their life to something that their own body did to them
I don't know if the thought of someone else makes me feel less lonely
Or just sadder at the thought that there are more people out there feeling the way that I do

What would I do if I could go back and talk to you
If I could go back and tell you what was coming
If I could warn you
If I could remind you to be strong, to be brave
And to fight for yourself
To remind you that you shouldn't define yourself by
the lessons of others
It is ok to define your own standards
Your own rules

Wake up child it's time for battle
I know you haven't slept for long
But warriors don't get to dream

Just hold on little one
I'm coming for you
I promise I won't let them forget you too

They say it takes a village to raise a child
But what if it takes an army to put that child back together
The adult that village burned needs warriors to be mended

Shake the dust from my soul

Blasting down doors I built up around myself

I was born in a storm of rage and pain
Hardened and built to withstand the weather
Shaped and nurtured by darkness and rain that felt like daggers
But somehow despite it all every once in awhile I could still catch a glimpse of a star or two

People say you should live each day like it's your last
But I don't agree with that
I want to live each day like it is my first
Before we were tainted by the world
Before our smiles were downturned
And the glint in our eyes began to diminish
Before we got used to hearing no and can't
Before we listened to others opinions over what we felt, within ourselves
Before we were silenced and taught what to say and do
When we were our purest and most raw
Naked, screaming, crying, amazing, and overwhelmed by the world we could see
When our eyes first opened
That is how I want to live

Floating just below the surface staring at the glow of
the sun that shines into the depths
The cold water
The warm glow
The silence
The floating
All ease my mind
The problem is that one can only hide beneath the
surface for so long
Until the burning in your lungs forces you to rejoin the
world
The burning that reminds me I am still here

Maybe it's okay to be broken
Broken promises reveal the truth
Broken bones reshape the body
Broken glass is somehow the most beautiful
And broken windows always let in more light

I guess all I can hope for is that one day when I look
back this will only be a short part of my story
And by writing it I will have become stronger

This book is a raw, honest, and thought provoking collection of poetry and prose aimed at promoting and creating deep, honest, and open dialogue on mental health, the struggles of mental illness, what it's like to love someone through it, and what it feels like to struggle with your own mind.  I hope that this book serves as a reminder to everyone that they are not alone in this world. Every time you hold this book, I want you to know that there is another person out there right now reading and living alongside of you.

Thank you to each and everyone one of you who takes the time to read my words, and to explore my journey through them. To you I am forever grateful. You have allowed me to come into your hearts and minds, and that is the most beautiful thing I can imagine.

www.ingramcontent.com/pod-product-compliance
Lightning Source LLC
Chambersburg PA
CBHW022108090426
42743CB00008B/758